Learning Tree 1 2 3

Magnets

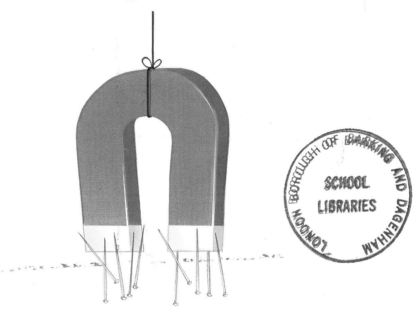

By Susan Baker

Illustrated by Mike Atkinson

CHERRYTREE BOOKS

Read this book and see if you can do the experiments and answer the questions. It will help if you have at least one small magnet. Ask an adult or an older friend to tell you if your answers are right or to help you if you find the questions difficult. Often there is more than one answer to a question.

A Cherrytree Book

Designed and produced by
A S Publishing

First published 1990
by Cherrytree Press Ltd
a subsidiary of
The Chivers Company Ltd
Windsor Bridge Road
Bath, Avon BA2 3AX

Copyright © Cherrytree Press Ltd 1990

British Library Cataloguing in Publication Data
Baker, Susan,
  Magnets.
  1. Magnets.
  I. Title   II. Atkinson, Michael   III. Series
  538.4

ISBN 0-7451-5093-4

Printed and bound in Italy by L.E.G.O. s.p.a., Vicenza

The cat has knocked over the pins.
How could you pick them up without
touching them?

You could pick them up with a magnet.

Magnets are very useful.
They will pick up pins, needles, paper clips
and anything else made of iron or steel.
They attract these metals.

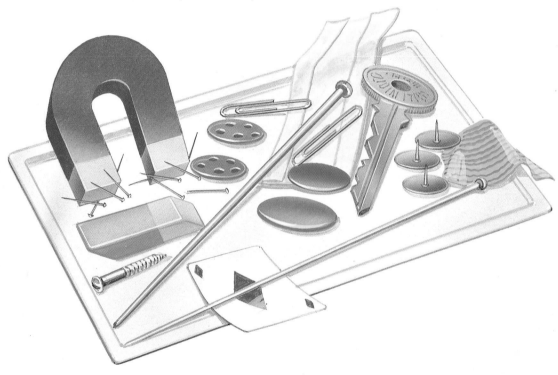

Collect a tray of small objects.
See what things cling to a magnet and what
things do not.

Go round your kitchen with a grown-up and
see what things a magnet sticks to.

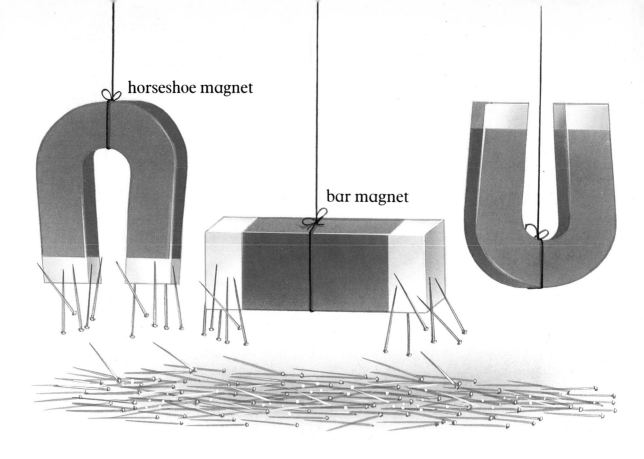

horseshoe magnet

bar magnet

Dangle a magnet over a pile of pins.
Where do most of the pins stick to it?

Every magnet has two ends called poles.
The magnetic force is strongest at the poles.
A horseshoe magnet is bent round so that the
poles are close together.

Each magnet has a north pole and a south pole.
They are marked N for north and S for south.

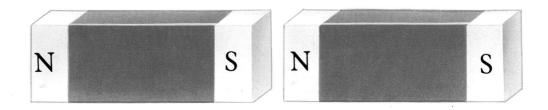

Put two magnets together end to end.
Do they stick together firmly or refuse to touch?

Turn one of the magnets round and try again.
What happens?

The pole of one magnet attracts the opposite pole of another. They stick firmly together.

A north pole attracts a south pole.

Put two south poles together and they push apart. Poles that are alike repel each other.

A north pole repels another north pole.

Remember, opposite poles attract, like poles repel.

These toy cars have magnets in them.
The two yellow cars have crashed.
The red car cannot catch the blue car.
Can you see why?

One magnet can make another magnet.

Hang a pin or paper clip from a magnet.
Pick up another pin with the tip of the first one.
Can you feel the pull as the second one is attracted to the first?

How many clips can you hang from the magnet?
Can you make a longer chain with a bigger magnet?

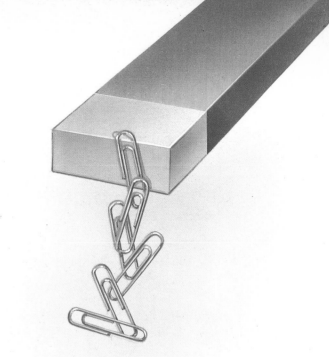

Slide the top pin of the chain away.
What happens?

Each pin or clip has been turned into a temporary magnet.

It will hold the next pin for a while but its magnetism will not last.

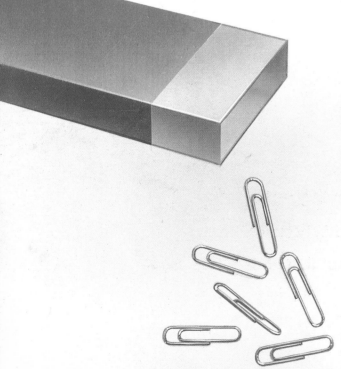

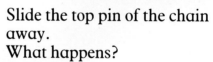

You can go fishing with magnets.
Use paper clips to make magnetic fish.
Tape a magnet to a string and see who can
pick up the most fish.

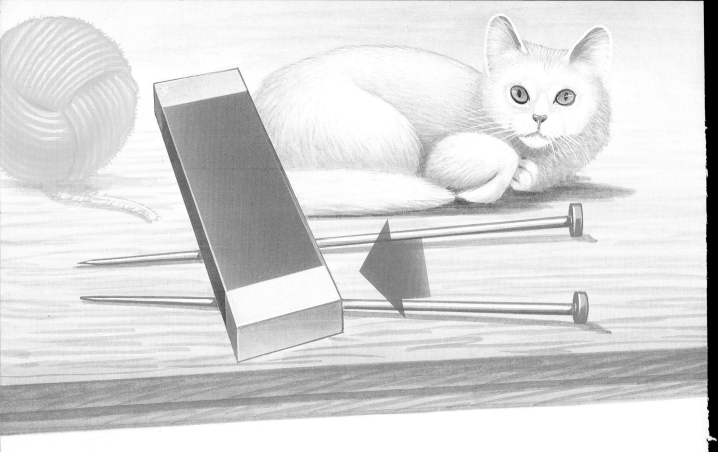

You can use one magnet to make another permanent magnet, one that will last. Magnetize a knitting needle or nail.
Stroke it from one end to the other with the pole of a magnet.
Always stroke it in the same direction, as you would stroke a cat.

How many strokes does it take to magnetize a nail?
Do more strokes make a stronger magnet?
What happens if you stroke the nail in the opposite direction?

You can weaken a magnet by dropping it or hitting it with a hammer.

Imagine that a magnet is filled with magnets.
Inside there are millions of tiny magnets.
All their poles point in the same direction.

When you drop the magnet, the little magnets
get jumbled up.
Their poles point in all directions and some
repel each other.
This makes the whole magnet weaker.

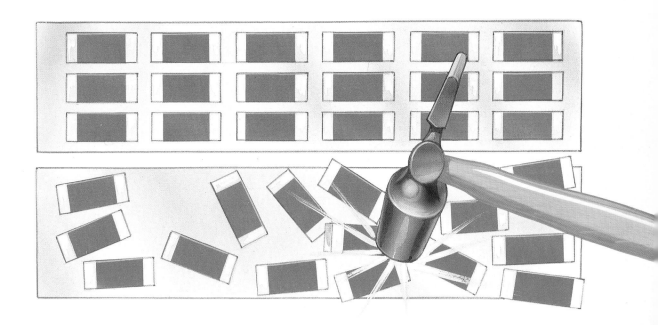

Heating a magnet harms it in the same way.
See if you can destroy the magnetism in one of
your home-made magnets. Be careful.

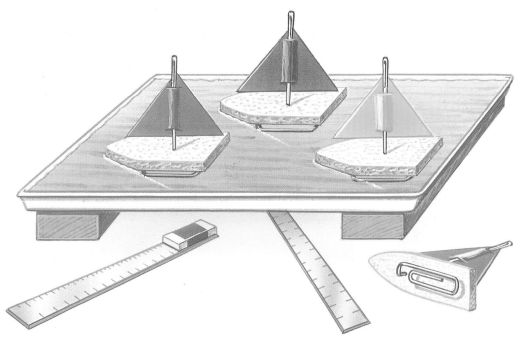

See if magnets work through water.
Make some little boats with needles stuck
through polystyrene.
Float the boats in a shallow tray of water.
Prop the tray up.

Tape a magnet to a ruler.
Slide it under the tray and see if you can move
the boats about.
Have races with your friends.

See if magnets work through other materials.
Put some nails inside a paper bag and some in
a plastic cup.
Slide a magnet along the outside of the bag or
cup and see if you can pull the nails out.
Try it with a tin can and a glass jar of water.

Mark an arrow on one of your magnets and
hang it up.
Which way does it hang when it stops swinging.
Move it to another place and see which way
the arrow points.

See how your magnet always points in the
same direction when it comes to rest.
The north pole points north.
The south pole points south, towards the sun.

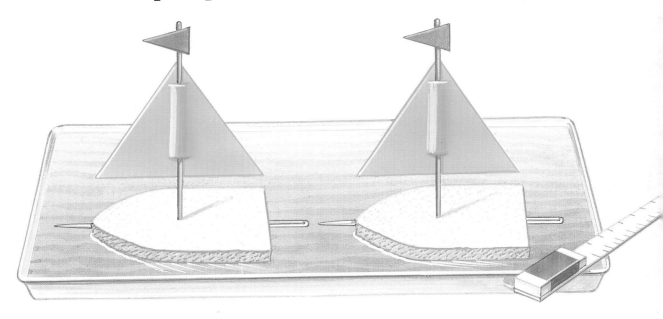

Magnetize some needles and make some more
boats with them.
Float them on water and see how they always
point the same way when they stop moving.
Can you make them sail in a line?

Because magnets always point the same way, people use them to find their way.
The needle of a compass is a swinging magnet.
It always points north/south.

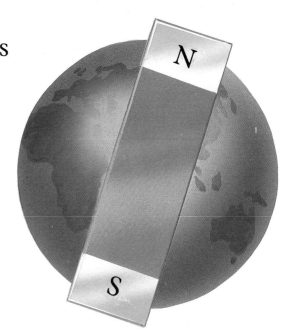

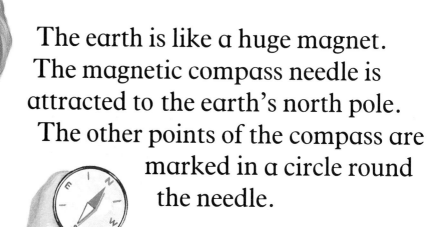

The earth is like a huge magnet.
The magnetic compass needle is attracted to the earth's north pole.
The other points of the compass are marked in a circle round the needle.

More about magnets

Magic stones
Magnetism was discovered in ancient times. People found stones that attracted metal and thought they were magic. The stones were made of a kind of metal called magnetite. It was a long time before scientists discovered the secret of the earth's magnetism.

Finding the way
The discovery of the earth's magnetism made the compass possible. Before the compass was invented, sailors had only the sun and stars to guide them when they were far from land.

The mystery of migration
Nobody knows for certain how birds find their way from one land to another when they migrate. They may be guided by the position of the sun. They may also be sensitive to the earth's magnetism.

Guard your magnets
Magnets affect other magnets. Do not play with your magnets near large metal objects like radiators.
Keep them away from calculators and other electronic equipment as they can stop them working.

Keep your bar magnets in pairs, with their opposite poles next to each other. They should have metal guards, or keepers, on the ends.

Tape recording
Magnetic tape is used to record sound. The tape is covered with tiny specks of metal. The recording machine reproduces sounds as a pattern of specks on the tape. When you play the tape, the cassette player converts the pattern back into sound.

Magnets and electricity
If wire is wound round a piece of iron, it will behave like a magnet when electricity is passed through the wire. It becomes an electromagnet.

Electromagnets can be switched on and off in an instant. A doorbell contains an electromagnet. When you ring the bell, the electric current flows through the wire. As soon as you take your finger off the button, the magnetism stops.

1

1 Draw a bar magnet and a horseshoe magnet on a piece of paper.

2 What are the ends of a magnet called?

3 What part of a magnet do pins stick to most?

4 Do magnets stick to glass?

5 Why do magnets stick to the fridge?

6 Which of the things in the picture will a magnet stick to?

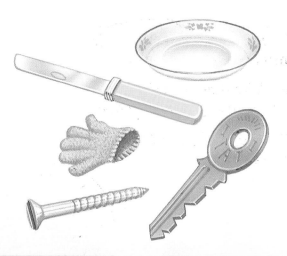

2

7 Keep a science notebook. Put the answers to these questions in it. Write down any questions you want to ask. Write down things you want to remember about magnets.

8 What could you use to find a needle in a haystack?

9 Which of these metals is magnetic: iron, brass or tin?

10 Will a magnet's north pole stick to a south pole?

11 Will a south pole stick to a south pole?

12 What does the word repel mean?

13 Will a paper wrapper stop a magnet from working?

14 What happens if you stroke a nail with the end of a magnet?

15 What do you use a compass for?

3

16 Which part of a compass is magnetic?

17 Name the four points of the compass.

18 Like poles repel. What do opposite poles do?

19 Would two north poles repel each other or attract?

20 Look for magnets in the kitchen. Look at doors, cupboards, fridges, knife racks, can openers and oven gloves. (Take care not to hurt yourself.) Make a list of any magnets you find.

21 Which of these materials will stop a magnet working: wood, water, a human hand?

22 Which way does a compass needle point?

23 Describe how a magnetic fishing game works.

24 Why might you find a magnet in a sewing basket?

25 How would you make a temporary magnet?

26 What happens when you hang up a magnet and let it swing?

27 Hang up a magnet so that it is swinging. Bring another magnet close up to each pole in turn. Describe what happens.

28 What happens if you stroke a nail with a magnet, first one way and then the other?

29 Electromagnets are used in doorbells. Find out where else they are used.

30 Why should you keep a magnet away from a computer?

31 What would you do to destroy a magnet?

Index